CHAPTER 1:
INTRODUCTION

11. How to Use This Guide

12. Overcoming Self-Doubt When Teaching a Language Imperfectly

CHAPTER 2:
FAMILY BASICS & EVERYDAY INTERACTIONS
Conceptos Básicos sobre la Familia e Interacciones Cotidianas

18. Common Nicknames & Terms of Endearment
Apodos Comunes y Términos Cariñosos

20. Regional Nicknames
Apodos Regionales

21. Basic Words & Phrases
Palabras y Frases Básicas

   Everyday Interactions
   Interacciones Cotidianas

   Exclamations
   Exclamaciones

Play
Jugar

Affection, Affirmation & Comfort
Afecto, Afirmación y Consuelo

Interacting with Others' Little Ones
Interactuar con los Pequeños de Otros

Give Direction
Dar Indicaciones

Classic Sayings
Dichos Típicos

Describe States & Behavior
Describir Estados y Comportamientos

CHAPTER 3:
PREGNANCY AND NEWBORN VOCABULARY
Vocabulario de Embarazo y Recién Nacidos

30. Newborn Necessities
Necesidades para Recién Nacidos

32. Pregnancy & Newborn Related Terminology
Terminología Relacionada con el Embarazo y los Recién Nacidos

34. Medical Terminology, Surrogacy & IVF-Related Phrases
Terminología Médica, Frases Relacionadas con la Gestación Subrogada y la FIV

36. Adoption
La Adopción

CHAPTER 4:
EARLY CHILDHOOD DEVELOPMENT AND ROUTINES
Desarrollo Infantil Temprano y Rutinas

40. Milestones
Logros del Desarrollo

41. Bedtime and Sleep
Hora de Acostarse y Sueño

43. Caregiving & Scheduling
Cuidado y Organización

45. First Phrases
Primeras Frases

CHAPTER 5: HEALTH AND HYGIENE
Salud e Higiene

48. Bathtime
La Hora del Baño

49. General Hygiene
Higiene General

50. Body Parts & Functions
Partes del Cuerpo y sus Funciones

52. Health
Salud

CHAPTER 6: EXPLORATION AND PLAY
Exploración y Juego

56. Playtime Vocabulary
Vocabulario para la Hora de Jugar

57. Reading
Lectura

58. Arts & Crafts
Manualidades y Arte

59. Picking Up Together
Recoger Juntos

60. At the Beach & Pool
La Playa y La Piscina

61. At the Park & Playground
Los Parques

63. Kids' Songs & Lullabies
Canciones Infantiles y Nanas

64. Kids' Characters
Personajes Infantiles

65. Sesame Street Characters
Personajes del Barrio Sésamo

CHAPTER 7:
FEEDING AND MEALTIME
Alimentación y Hora de Comer

68. Common Food-Related Phrase
Frases Comunes Relacionadas con la Comida

69. Feeding Tools and Methods
Herramientas y Métodos para la Alimentación

70. Kid-Friendly Foods - American
Comidas para Niños - EEUU

71. Kid-Friendly Foods - Spain
Comidas para Niños - España

CHAPTER 8:
SEASONAL AND CULTURAL EVENTS
Eventos Estacionales y Culturales

75. Birthdays
Los Cumpleaños

75. Halloween

76. Christmas and the Three Kings
La Navidad y Los Reyes Magos

80. New Year's Eve
La Noche Vieja

CHAPTER 9:
PHRASES TO GUIDE KIDS' BEHAVIOR
Frases para guiar el comportamiento infantil

84. Basic Behavioral Vocabulary
Vocabulario básico del Comportamiento Infantil

85. Managing Tough Situations
Navegando Situaciónes Difíciles

86. Words of Affirmation
Palabras de Afirmación

88. Establishing Clear Expectations
Estableciendo Expectativas Claras

89. Recognizing Emotions
Reconociendo las Emociones

90. Redirecting Behavior
Redirigiendo el Comportamiento

91. Reinforcing Good Behavior
Reforzando el Buen Comportamiento

92. Calm Consequences
Consecuencias Tranquilas

93. Encourage Reflection
Fomentando la Reflexión

94. Empathy & Connection
Empatía y Conexión

95. Apologizing
Más Opciones para Decir "Lo Siento"

96. Managing Tantrums
Navegando Rabietas

97. Bedtime Struggles
Dificultades a la Hora de Dormir

CHAPTER 10: RECETAS PARA LA FAMILIA

100. Pan con tomate
101. Puree de calabaza y zanahoria
102. Tortilla española al estilo mamá
104. Huevos rotos rápidos
105. Carne navideña al estilo Ursula

CHAPTER 11: APPENDIX

108. The 3+1 Rules of Pronunciation
119. My Favorite Social Media Resources

CHAPTER 12: TRAVEL TIPS: SPAIN WITH KIDS

114. Timing
114. Parks, Parks, Parks
115. Dining
116. What I Stock Up On In Spain
118. Transportation
119. Medical Aid

Introduction

ALEX CRONIN

Hi, I'm Alex. I grew up in the Chicagoland area with parents who, while native English speakers, each know a foreign language. I became the family's only Spanish speaker, starting my journey in 4th grade and nurturing it through four study abroad experiences beginning at 16.

My time in Spain not only made me conversationally fluent but also gave me a second "family"—friends in Madrid who welcome me like one of their own, even now when I visit them every year.

When I was pregnant, I knew I wanted my daughter to grow up bilingual, speaking Spanish as well or better than I do. To make that happen, I committed to speaking to her exclusively in Spanish.

But I quickly realized that while I was comfortable chatting with adults, I lacked the **basic vocabulary for parenting in Spanish**: feeding, diaper changes, and playtime. Google Translate and help from my Spanish family became my lifelines.

Now, with a two-year-old at home, I've compiled this book for parents like me—**non-native Spanish speakers dreaming of raising bilingual children**. While many terms in this book are universal across Spanish-speaking countries, it's especially tailored for those who plan to interact with Spaniards.

I hope it saves you time and brings joy to your bilingual parenting journey!

ALEXIA LEROY

Hi, I'm Alexia. Born and raised in Paris, France, I studied English and Spanish throughout middle and high school.

I've always been fascinated by languages and the way they open doors **to connect with people from all over the world**. Since I was a kid, I've always wanted to live abroad and explore new cultures.

In college, I had the chance to study in Madrid for six months and instantly **fell in love with the city and the vibrant Spanish culture**.

A few years later, **I moved to Chicago** to study graphic design and ended up staying for three years. That's actually where I met Alex, we were both working at the same marketing agency!

To this day, living in the U.S. has been one of the most transformative experiences of my life. It truly deepened my appreciation for **the power of language and cross-cultural exchange**.

When Alex told me about this book, **I knew I wanted to be part of the journey. It brings together so many things I love: travel, language, and storytelling**.

I had so much fun bringing her words to life through design and **adding my own creative touch to her story**.

You can check out my work at **www.letszigzag.com**

How to use this guide

This book is intended to provide intermediate-level Spanish learners with common terminology used when talking with or about young children.

While many of these words are ones I learned from my Spanish "family," this has also been reviewed by professors who are Spanish natives.

Why Spain? I wanted to be sure to capture colloquialisms and common phrases for those of us who plan to **build relationships with our Spanish friends and loved ones**, and/or those who are planning to spend a lot of time in the country with their kids.

I have added some **cultural insights** about certain terms and phrases that shine light on some of the beautiful differences in language and culture I've learned over the years.

This guide is by no means exhaustive, but I hope it serves as a **quick reference guide so I can save you countless hours of researching**.

Overcoming Self-Doubt When Teaching a Language Imperfectly

There's a scene in one of my favorite TV shows, *The Office*, where one of the main characters, Dwight, is on the search for a day laborer. His conversation with a character we know to be a native English-speaker goes like this:

Nate: Hola amigo.

Dwight: Hola. Eres un bueno worker?

Nate: Si, yo muy bueno worker.

Dwight: Y el acento, donde are you from?

Nate: Scranton. Y before that, la Philadelphia.

Dwight: You speak English?

Nate: Yes, I'm really good at English.

Dwight: Ok, me too, get in the car.

There are some days I watch this and cringe at more than just the cultural insensitivity of the scene. I cringe wondering if this is how my daughter and I will sound to others. In reality, I know her Spanish is already on track to be better than this example, and I'm certain mine is. However, there are days when I feel self-conscious and embarrassed that I am teaching her very imperfect Spanish.

I made **a conscious decision to stop caring about this**. Here's why.

When I travel with my English-speaking parents and daughter to see my "family" in Spain, my parents are overjoyed by my ability to communicate with just about anyone I meet. They don't know my Spanish is far from perfect and that I make frequent mistakes; **all they see is someone who is effectively communicating in any situation**. I can understand and be understood. I can carry on a conversation.

From their perspective, **they would *love* to be able to speak like I do**. Even though I often conjugate verbs wrong and don't always have "concordancia de numero, género y tiempo," **I am able to move about the world and make connections in a way they can't**.

Most native speakers I have encountered in my studies and travels **do not focus on my errors, but rather they focus on my abilities**. Instead of rolling their eyes at all my mistakes or refraining from conversation because I don't conjugate verbs like a master, **they are delighted to chat** and often ask me a lot of questions.

This will seem funny to most, but I am guessing many of you reading this may relate: I enjoy taking cabs and Ubers in Spain because **I often receive positive feedback on my language skills** during the ride. It's so common for cab drivers to remark on my ability to converse and ask me how I learned Spanish that my loved ones have heard my response a million times and it makes us all smile. These cab rides give me a boost of confidence.

This process has a powerful snowball effect: the more I speak with native speakers, the more people help and correct me, the more I learn, the better I speak, and the more confident I become. Rinse and repeat. I've been doing some version of this for almost twenty years.

Learning Spanish will be a lifelong journey for me. I'm virtually certain I will never, ever be mistaken for a native speaker. And that's ok!

My Spanish family also helps me in every conversation we have. One of the ways my Spanish "family" helps me to continue to improve my Spanish is by **welcoming me to converse with them naturally** while they frequently but gently correct me. When I pause or stumble, they fill in the blank. When I use a wrong word, they just say the right word as I continue my thought. Or, they restate my sentence in a better way and then continue with their response. There's no judgement. **There's no pressure. There's only support**. That's a framework I want to emulate at home.

I see content on social media all the time that coaches parents to focus on what their kids *can* do when framing important lessons.

For example, @*transformingmotherhood* posted a video on December 7, 2024 that she titled "magnify strengths," and captioned it,

"Before you criticize, start by stating the strength you know is deep down in there that maybe wasn't showing in the moment. Always remind your child of their goodness and they will start to believe it too."

I recommend looking up this video because **the examples she gives are really illuminating**, and I think you'll see the same parallels I did to learning a new language. My best "teachers" have been **those who encourage me and focus on what I'm doing right**, which has built my confidence and made me a sponge for any and all corrections.

These experiences are what I try to remind myself of when I get frustrated, filled with self-doubt, or am feeling self-conscious that I'm teaching my daughter less-than-perfect Spanish. If the most I can ever help her achieve is an approximation of my level, I'll be proud.

My hope is that this guide will help you in some way, wherever you are on your linguistic journey.

Family Basics & Everyday Interactions

Conceptos Básicos sobre la Familia
e Interacciones Cotidianas

COMMON NICKNAMES & TERMS OF ENDEARMENT
Apodos Comunes y Términos Cariñosos

NICKNAMES FOR FAMILY MEMBERS
Apodos para los Miembros de la Familia

Papis Parents

Abu Grandma or grandpa (short for "abuela/abuelo")

Tita Aunt

Titi Aunt or Uncle (playful)

Tito Uncle

Hermani Brother or Sister (playful, from hermano/hermana)

Hermanito/Hermanita (younger brother/sister)

PET NAMES FOR YOUR LITTLE ONE
Apodos Cariñosos para tus Peques

Cariño Sweetie

Cari Sweetie

Mi amor My love

Amorcito Sweet love

Gordi Chubs *(in a kind way)*

Peque Little one
This term can also be used as a general term for kids. "Hay un parque para los peques por aquí?"

Chiqui Little one

Cielo Darling. *Literal translation: "Sky"*

Vida mía My life

Solete Little sunshine

Rey/Reina King/Queen

Tesoro Treasure

Churri Sweetie *(informal and playful)*

Muñeco/Muñeca Doll

Pitu Cutie *(common in Asturias)*

Bombón Sweetie, *literal translation "chocolate bonbon"*

Cosita Little thing

Nano/Nana Buddy/Little one
(common in Valencia and Catalonia)

Pitufa/Pitufo Smurf
(used for small children)

Chiquitín/Chiquitina Little one *(diminutive)*

Bicho Little rascal *(affectionate in this context. Can be negative in other contexts)*

Ratoncito/Ratoncita Little mouse

Travieso/Traviesa Mischievous one

REGIONAL NICKNAMES
Apodos Regionales

Txiki
Petita
Rapaciña

CATALAN
Petita/Petit Little one
Nena/Nen Girl/boy
Xiqueta/Xiquet Little girl/boy
(used in Valencia)

GALICIAN
Neniña/Neniño Little girl/boy
Rapaciña/Rapaciño Little kid

ASTURIAS
Guaje Kid

BASQUE
Txiki Little one
Maitia Darling/Love

BASIC WORDS & PHRASES
Palabras y Frases Básicas

EVERYDAY INTERACTIONS
Interacciones Cotidianas

¿Te vienes? Are you coming?

¿Qué me cuentas?
How are you? What's going on?

Ni fu, ni fa So so *(about how you're feeling, how something tastes, etc)*

¡Voy! I'm on my way! Coming!

¡Me piro! I'm taking off!

Muy amable That's kind of you

No hay de que You're welcome, don't mention it

Con gusto You're welcome, with pleasure

Con mucho cariño You're welcome

¡Hasta mañana, iguana!
See you tomorrow, iguana!

Qué tengas un buen día, ardilla!
Have a good day, squirrel!

Nos vemos al ratito, patito
See you soon, little duck

Me parto. That's hilarious

¿Te apuntas? Are you in? Are you up for it?

No te sigo I don't understand, I'm not following

No lo pillo I don't get it

Venga
Alright, come on, let's go, c'mon, yeah right

EXCLAMATIONS
Exclamaciones

Mola That's cool! / I like it

Guay Cool

¡Qué chulo! Cool!

¡Qué chuli! Cool/cute

¡Hala! Wow!

¡Vaya! Wow! No way!

¡Qué va! No way!

¡Madre mía! Wow! Goodness!

¡Qué moni! How cute!

¡Qué majo! He's so nice!

¡Ay, esa pupita! Ouchie, boo boo

Ups Oopsy

¡Uy, cuidado! Oopsy daisy

PLAY
Jugar

¡Cucutrás! Peekaboo

¡Choca! High five

¡Cuchi cuchi! Tickling sound (playful)

Hacer pedorretas To blow raspberries

AFFECTION, AFFIRMATION & COMFORT
Afecto, Afirmación y Consuelo

¿Quieres un abrazo?
Do you want a hug?

¡Ven aquí, mi peque!
Come here, my little one!

Dame un besito Give me a kiss

No pasa nada, cariño
It's okay, sweetheart

¿Dónde está tu peluche?
Where's your stuffed animal?

Cuenta conmigo Count on me

¡Tú puedes! You can do it!

¡Bravo! Well done

¡Chapó! Well done

¡Grande! Well done

Olé Well done

Bien hecho Well done

Buen trabajo Good work

Te aplaudo de pie Congrats!

Agacharse To bend down

Ponerse a su altura
To crouch to a kid's level

Acurrucarse
To snuggle with someone

Achuchar
To cuddle

INTERACTING WITH OTHERS' LITTLE ONES
Interactuar con los Pequeños de Otros

¡Está muy espabilada! She is very alert! *(This is a common compliment/observation made of newborns and babies)*

¡Qué grande te estás haciendo! You're getting so big!

¡Qué fuertote estas! You are getting strong!

Estas hecho todo un hombre/toda una mujer
You are just like a grown up

¡Cómo has crecido! You've grown up so much!

¡Es una monada! He/she is so cute!

¡Qué moni/mono! How cute!

¡Qué rico! How cute!

GIVE DIRECTION
Dar Indicaciones

Toma Here, take this

Vamos Let's go

Agarra mi mano Take my hand, hold onto my hand

¡Ojo! Take note, watch out, pay attention

¡Para! Stop! *[physical movement, as in stop walking]*

¡Basta! Stop it! *(hitting, yelling)*

Quédate aquí/ahí Wait here/there

Espera Hold on, wait

Te he dicho que no I've repeatedly said no

¡Suelta! Let go

¡Venga, vamos todos!
A way to get kids to follow you or get going

¡Caracol, caracol, todos en control
A way to ask kids to calm/quiet down

Hada, hada, ahora no digo nada
A way to ask kids to stop talking

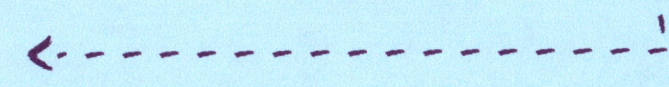

CLASSIC SAYINGS
Dichos Típicos

De tal palo, tal astilla
The apple doesn't fall far from the tree

A otra cosa, mariposa
Let's change the subject
Next topic, please
Let's move along

Cuesta un ojo de la cara
It costs an arm and a leg

No hay mal que por bien no venga
Every cloud has a silver lining

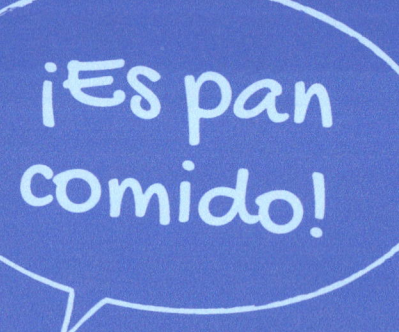

¡Es pan comido!
It's a piece of cake

Es mano de santo
It works like a charm

En un plis plas
In the blink of an eye

En un abrir y cerrar los ojos
In the blink of an eye

Más vale tarde que nunca
Better late than never

Quien la sigue, la consigue
If at first you don't succeed, try again

No es oro todo lo que reluce
All that glitters is not gold

DESCRIBE STATES & BEHAVIOR
Describir Estados y Comportamiento

Está en su salsa She's in her element

Estar en las nubes
To be in love or distracted, to have your head in the clouds

Ser un aguafiestas To be a party pooper

Es más bueno/a que el pan He/she is super kind
(literally: better than bread)

Está como una cabra He/she is acting crazy (in a fun way)

Se te va la olla You're bananas! (in a nice way)

Estar hecho un cuadro To be a mess
"Qué hiciste, mi amor? Estás hecho un cuadro!"

Pregnancy and Newborn Vocabulary

Vocabulario de Embarazo y Recién Nacidos

NEWBORN NECESSITIES

Necesidades para Recién Nacidos

Las toallitas húmedas Wet wipes

Los pañales Diapers

Los dodotis/pañales dodot Diapers
Note: Dodot is a brand like Pampers. In Spain, this brand name is often used interchangeably for any diaper regardless of brand, similar to how Americans use the term Kleenex when referring to facial tissues.

Pañal reutilizable Cloth diapers

Pañal de tela Cloth diapers

El chupete Binky, pacifier

Crema pañal Diaper cream

El arrullo Swaddle
Ojo: swaddling is not a common practice in Spain and is often met with confusion or even concern for the baby.

El body Onesie

Hamaca Baby bouncer

El bote para pañales Diaper pail

Carrito Stroller

La cuna de viaje Travel crib

Cuna de viaje Pack and Play

Portabebés Baby carrier/harness

El fular portabebés Baby sling

Silla de coche Car seat

El mordedor Teething ring

El andador Walker

Dormir al bebé / Acostar al bebé To put a baby down [to sleep] / to get a baby down to sleep
E.g. La duermo a las 8. – I put her down [to go to sleep] at 8
La voy a dormir – I'm going to put her down

PREGNANCY & NEWBORN RELATED TERMINOLOGY

Terminología Relacionada con el Embarazo y los Recién Nacidos

Es una nena It's a girl!

Es un nene/chico It's a boy!

Será niño/a It's a girl/boy

Antojos Cravings

Náuseas matutinas Morning sickness

La prueba de embarazo Pregnancy test

El parto en casa Home birth

La matrona/partera Midwife

La Doula Doula

¡Es una nena!

¡Es un chico!

La fecha probable de parto
Due date

Mi fecha de parto es el [fecha]
I'm due on [date]

El trimestre Trimester

Romper aguas To break water

Acabo de romper aguas
My water just broke

Las contracciones Contractions

Dar a luz To give birth

El peso al nacer Birth weight

El extractor de leche Breast pump

La lactancia materna Breastfeeding

Hacer eructar To burp a baby

Envolver To swaddle

MEDICAL TERMINOLOGY, SURROGACY & IVF-RELATED PHRASES

Terminología Médica, Frases Relacionadas con la Gestación Subrogada y la FIV

La cesárea C-section

El saco amniótico Amniotic sack

El cordón umbilical Umbilical cord

La transferencia embrionaria Embryo transfer

El embarazo por subrogación Surrogate pregnancy

La gestación subrogada Surrogacy

La madre subrogada Surrogate mother

El vientre de alquiler Surrogate *(colloquial, less formal)*

Los futuros padres Intended parents

La fertilización in vitro (FIV) In vitro fertilization *(IVF)*

La clínica de fertilidad Fertility clinic

El ciclo de FIV IVF cycle

La ecografía Ultrasound

El monitor fetal Fetal monitor

La epidural Epidural

El parto natural Natural birth

La punción ovárica Egg retrieval

La inseminación artificial Artificial insemination

La transferencia de embriones frescos/congelados Fresh/frozen embryo transfer

El tratamiento de fertilidad Fertility treatment

La infertilidad Infertility

La betaespera The waiting period after embryo transfer

El resultado positivo/negativo Positive/negative result

El aborto espontáneo/pérdida del bebé Miscarriage

Estamos en tratamiento de fertilidad We are undergoing fertility treatment

Estamos buscando una madre subrogada We are looking for a surrogate mother

El tratamiento está funcionando The treatment is working

Hemos congelado embriones para el futuro We have frozen embryos for the future

La betaespera es muy difícil emocionalmente. The waiting period is very emotionally difficult

Estamos esperando la transferencia embrionaria We are waiting for the embryo transfer

Nuestro bebé es fruto de la FIV Our baby is the result of IVF

Estamos agradecidos por nuestra gestante We are grateful for our surrogate

Es un proceso lleno de esperanza y paciencia It's a process full of hope and patience

El embarazo múltiple Multiple pregnancy
(in case twins or multiples are involved)

ADOPTION
La Adopción

Adoptar / Ser adoptado(a)
To adopt / To be adopted

La familia adoptiva Adoptive family

La familia biológica / La familia de origen
Birth (biological) family

Los trámites de adopción
The legal/administrative steps involved in the adoption process

El expediente de adopción
Adoption file/paperwork

El acogimiento familiar Foster care
(temporary placement before or instead of formal adoption)

El juicio de adopción
Adoption hearing *(legal court process)*

El certificado de nacimiento
Birth certificate *(which may be reissued after adoption)*

El libro de familia Family record book in Spain *(official document where children's legal status is recorded)*

"He crecido en una familia adoptiva que me ha dado todo su cariño" "I've grown up in an adoptive family that has given me so much love"

"Siento mucha curiosidad por conocer mi historia de origen" "I'm very curious to learn about my birth story/roots"

"Estoy muy agradecido(a) por la oportunidad que me han dado" "I'm really grateful for the opportunity they've given me"

"**Fue un proceso largo, pero mereció la pena**"
"It was a long process, but it was worth it"

"**Para mí, ellos son mis verdaderos padres**"
"For me, they are my real parents"

"**Hubo que reunir mucha documentación para completar los trámites**" "We had to gather a lot of paperwork to finish the process"

"**La entrevista con los psicólogos y trabajadores sociales fue importante**" "The interview with psychologists and social workers was important"

"**A veces me pregunto cómo sería mi familia de origen**" "Sometimes I wonder what my birth family is like"

"**Ha sido una experiencia única que me ha marcado profundamente**" "It's been a unique experience that's profoundly shaped me"

"**Mis padres adoptivos me dieron un hogar y una educación fantástica**" "My adoptive parents gave me a home and a fantastic upbringing"

"Sentí mucha inseguridad cuando era más joven, pero ahora lo llevo bien"
"I felt very uncertain when I was younger, but now I handle it well"

"Hay días en los que necesito hablar de mis orígenes, y otros en los que no"
"There are days when I need to talk about my roots, and others when I don't"

Early Childhood Development and Routines

Desarrollo Infantil Temprano y Rutinas

MILESTONES
Logros del Desarrollo

Gatear To crawl

Ponerse de pie To stand up

Los primeros pasos First steps

Saludar To wave

Dientes de leche Baby teeth

Balbucear To babble

Decir sus primeras palabras To say their first words

Applaudir To clap your hands

Guiñar un ojo To wink

Asentir To nod yes

Los primeros pasos

BEDTIME AND SLEEP
Hora de Acostarse y Sueño

BEDTIME ITEMS
Artículos para la Hora de Dormir

La cuna Crib

El moisés Bassinet

La mecedora Rocking chair

El humidificador Humidifier

El vigilabebés/monitor de bebé Baby monitor

Saco de dormir Sleep sack

El protector de colchón Mattress protector

La luz de noche Nightlight

La máquina de ruido blanco White noise machine

SLEEP ROUTINE
Rutina para Dormir

Acunar a To rock
Ejemplo: Le canté una nana [a mi hijo] mientras lo acunaba entre mis brazos.

Arropar To tuck in *"Te arroparé antes de dormir"*

Mecer a To rock

Las nanas/Las canciones de cuna
Lullabies

Cantarle a alguien para dormir
To sing someone to sleep

Tener problemas para dormirse
To have trouble falling asleep

La rutina para ir a la cama
Bedtime routine

Es la hora de dormir
It's bedtime

El horario de sueño
Sleep schedule

El balanceo
Rocking motion

Dormir juntos
To co-sleep

No conseguir dormir
To be unable to sleep

Pasar la noche despierto
To stay up all night

La siesta
Naptime

Es la hora de siesta
It's naptime

Dormirse en brazos
To fall asleep in arms

Balada de cuna Rockabye

¡A mimir! Time to sleep *(child-friendly)*

¡Buenos días, dormilón/dormilona!
Good morning, sleepyhead!

¡Es la hora de las gallinas!
It's so early!

Son las tantas
It's way past bedtime

CAREGIVING & SCHEDULING
Cuidado y Organización

La guardería Daycare

Niñero/a Babysitter

La mochila de la guardería Daycare backpack

La fiambrera Lunchbox

Echarse una siesta To nap

Merienda Snack time

El menú de la guardería Daycare menu

La hora de comer Lunch time

→ **En la guardería, comen a las 12** At daycare, lunchtime is at 12

→ **Comemos a la una** We eat lunch at 1

→ **Qué has comido para el almuerzo?** What did you have for lunch?

La hora de siesta Nap time

→ **Es la hora de siesta, cariño!** It's nap time, sweetie!

→ **Hace siesta entre las 11.00-13.00**

→ **Se echa la siesta entre las 11.00-13.00**

Hora de cenar
Dinner time

→ **Ahora cenamos**
It's dinnertime

→ **Cenamos a las 6**
We eat dinner at 6

La hora de dormir/ ir a la cam Bed time

→ **Se acuesta a las 7:30**
Her bed time is 7:30

Un guión para explicar la rutina diaria

Vamos a hablar de lo que **hacemos todos los días**, ¿vale?

Por la mañana, **nos despertamos** y **desayunamos juntos**. Después, nos lavamos las manos y los dientes y nos vestimos para **ir a la guardería**.

En la guardería, vas a jugar con tus amigos y **aprender cosas nuevas**. Por la mañana tendrás un momento para **la merienda** y después será hora de escuchar cuentos. Luego saldrás para jugar al aire libre.

Cuando vuelvas de afuera, ya será **la hora de comer** y, después, todos se echarán una siesta. Al despertarte, tendrás más tiempo para **jugar con tus amigos** y leer libros con tu profe.

Y antes de que te des cuenta, **¡ya estaré allí para recogerte!** Volvemos a casa o vamos al parque.

A las seis y media, cenaremos. Después de la cena, llegará la hora del baño, **¡qué divertido!** Cuando termines el baño, nos pondremos el pijama, **leeremos unos libros juntos**, y después, a la cama para dormir.

FIRST PHRASES

Primeras Frases

Cógelo Pick it up

Sujétalo Hold it

Vamos allá
Let's go there

Cuidado Careful

Suéltalo Let go

Dámelo Give it to me

Abrocha el cinturon
Buckle your seatbelt

Lo hago yo mismo
I'll do it myself

Salta alto Jump high

¡Lo has hecho muy bien!
You did great!

¡Lo has hecho muy bien!

Salta alto

Health and Hygiene

Salud e Higiene

BATHTIME
La Hora del Baño

La bañera Bathtub

Temperatura del agua
Water temperature

→ **El agua está calentito**
The water is warm

→ **Está caliente!**
It's too hot!

La esponja Sponge

Mete los pies primero
Put your feet in first

Champú Shampoo

Gel de baño para bebé
Baby body wash

La toallita
Washcloth

Aclarar To rinse

Ten cuidado, no salpiques demasiado
Be careful, don't splash too much

El patito de goma Rubber duck

Burbujas Bubbles

Jugar con espuma
Play with foam/bubbles

Vamos a llenar la bañera
Let's fill the bathtub

GENERAL HYGIENE
Higiene General

Tomar un baño To take a bath

Lavarse los manos y la cara To wash your hands & face

Cepillarse los dientes To brush your teeth

Pañales de subir y bajar Pull-ups *(diapers)*

Limpiarse el culete To wipe your bum

El aspirador nasal Nasal aspirator

El peine Comb

El cepillo Brush

El gel de ducha Bodywash

La crema hidratante infantil Baby moisturizer

El cortauñas para bebés Baby nail clippers

El perfume de bebé Baby perfume
Cultural note: It's common in Spain for people to spritz their children's clothes with perfume as part of their "getting ready" routine at home or at daycare. You'll find baby and kids perfumes in the kids section of popular stores like Zara and Mango.

Los kikis Pigtails
(cuidado: "kiki" tiene otro significado – "echar un kiki" is "to have a quickie")

⟶ **Quieres que te haga kikis/coletas?** Do you want pigtails?

La coleta Ponytail

Los moños Buns (hairstyle)

Las trenzas Braids

Una goma Hair tie

La diadema Headband

Cherokí Mohawk (hairstyle)

BODY PARTS & FUNCTIONS
Partes del Cuerpo y sus Funciones

Pipí Pee pee

Caca Poop

La diarrea Diarrhea

Estar estreñido To be constipated

El culito, culete o culín Bum

Oloroso Stinky

La barriga/La tripita Tummy

Entrenamiento para ir al baño Potty training

Asiento de entrenamiento Potty training stool

El váter Toilet

Los cachetes/Las mejillas Cheeks

Un eructo Burp

Sonarse la nariz To blow one's nose
example: Por favor, suénate la nariz, cariño.

Un pedo Fart

El ombligo Belly button

El pene/la colita Penis

La vagina/el chichi Vagina

Potar To vomit (colloquial)

El útero Uterus

Vamos a cambiarte el pañal Let's change your diaper

¿Tienes ganas de ir al baño? Do you feel like going to the bathroom?

Vamos al baño
Let's go to the potty

¿Te sientas en el váter?
Do you want to sit on the toilet?

Es hora de hacer pipí/caca
It's time to pee/poop

¿Tienes que hacer caca?
Do you need to poop?

¿Quieres hacer pipí?
Do you need to pee?

¿Necesitas ayuda para limpiarte?
Do you need help wiping?

¿Tienes el pañal sucio?
Do you have a poopy diaper?

¿Necesitas ir al baño?
Do you need to go potty?

¿Quieres usar el orinal?
Do you need to go potty?
(specifically on the potty chair)

¿Te has tirado un pedo?
Did you fart?

¿Tienes que eructar?
Do you have to burp?

Vamos a lavarte el culito
Let's clean your bum

Voy a ponerte crema en el culito
I'll put cream on your bum

Lávate las manos después de hacer pipí
Wash your hands after peeing

¡Qué culito tan limpio!
What a clean bum!

¿Te limpio los mocos?
May I get your boogers?

HEALTH

Salud

Una pupita
Ouchie, boo-boo

El moco Boogers

Estar mal(a) To be sick

Tener tos To have a cough

Tener mocos
To have a runny nose

Estar constipado
To be constipated

Tener la nariz taponada
To have a stuffy nose

La dermatitis del pañal
Diaper rash

El aspirador nasal.
Nasal aspirator

Una pupa
Small injury/scratch

Un moretón Bruise

Los escalofríos Chills

La dentición Teething (phase)

Echa los dientes He/she is teething

La solución salina Saline solution

Un rasguño A scratch

Una pupita

Un moretón

Los escalofríos

El dolor de barriga
Stomachache

Las tiritas BandAids

Las gasas Gauze

El termómetro digital
Digital thermometer

El termómetro infrarrojo
Infrared thermometer

La pomada antibiótica
Antibiotic ointment

Exploration and Play

Exploración y Juego

PLAYTIME VOCABULARY

Vocabulario para la Hora de Jugar

La alfombra de juegos Play mat

Osito de peluche Teddy bear

El tren de juguete Toy train

Los juguetes apilables Stacking toy

La pizarra magnética Magnetic board

La casa de muñecas Dollhouse

La cuerda para saltar Jump rope

Los coches de juguete Toy cars

El gimnasio para bebés Baby gym

Cubo para clasificar formas Shape sorter *(box)*

La plastilina Playdough

Las marionetas Puppets

El tobogán Slide

La bici / bicicleta Bicycle

El columpio Swing

El triciclo Tricycle

El patinete Scooter

Hacer pompas To blow a bubble *(of gum or from a wand)*

Patea la pelota Kick the ball

¡Cógela! Catch it!

Tira la pelota Throw the ball

Rebota el balón Bounce the ball

READING
Lectura

Los libros de tela Cloth books

Los libros de cartón Board books

Los cuentos para dormir Bedtime stories

El cuento Story or tale

El libro de actividades Activity book

La caperucita roja Little Red Riding Hood

La oruga muy hambrienta
The Hungry, Hungry Caterpillar

¿Quieres que te lea un cuento?
Do you want me to read you a story?

Vamos a leer antes de dormir
Let's read before going to bed

¿Qué libro quieres leer hoy?
What book do you want to read today?

El Pollo Pepe

A very popular Spanish children's book character, el Pollo Pepe is one of the most recognizable and foundational characters in Spanish children's literature.

ARTS & CRAFTS
Manualidades y Arte

Las ceras Crayons

Los rotuladores Markers

La cartulina Cardstock

La purpurina Glitter

El pegamento de barra Glue stick

Las pegatinas Stickers

Pintura de dedos Finger paints

Plastilina Playdough

El pincel Brush

Las limpiapipas Pipe cleaners

Pegar To glue

Salpicar To splatter *(paint or water)*

Aplastar To flatten or press down

Arrugar To crumple

Espolvorear To sprinkle

Plastificar To laminate

Firmar To sign one's name

¡A recoger!

PICKING UP TOGETHER

Recoger Juntos

Guárdalo, por favor

Recoger To pick things up, tidy up

Recógelo, por favor Pick it up please

La aspiradora The vacuum

Pasar la aspiradora To vacuum

La escoba Broom

Barrer To sweep

Fregar Wash *(the floor or dishes)*

Lavar Clean

El cubito (o cubo) Bucket

Ordenado Tidy

La mancha Stain

Frotar To scrub

Desordenado Messy

El trapo Rag

¡A recoger! Let's clean up

Guárdalo, por favor Put it away please

AT THE BEACH & POOL
La Playa y La Piscina

La pisci / piscina Pool

El flotador Floatie

Los chorizos Water spouts/ fountains as in a splash pad

Hacer un castillo de arena To build a sand castle

El cubo, palas para arena, el colador y las moldes Bucket, shovels, strainer, molds

Cavar To dig

Salpicar To splash

Gafas de sol Sunglasses

Buscar tesoro Treasure hunt

Sombrilla Beach umbrella

Sombrerito Hat

Sombra Shadow

Cangrejo Crab

Crema solar Sunscreen

Medusa Jellyfish

Tiburón Shark

Delfín Dolphin

AT THE PARK & PLAYGROUND

Los Parques

Note: In most parts of Spain, there are **tons of playgrounds**. Many playgrounds are even **adjacent to bars and restaurants** so parents can relax and chat while kids play.

Many Spanish parents **connect with one another** at parks and have a caña instead of hovering over their kids (age dependent, of course).

Parque infantil Playground

Patio Schoolyard, school playground
E.g. Todos los niños salieron al patio durante el recreo.

Tobogán Slide

¿Quieres bajar el tobogán?
Do you want to go down the slide?

¿Quieres que baje contigo?
Do you want me to go down with you?

Columpios Swings

Quieres ir a los columpios?
Do you want to go on the swings?

Pasamanos Monkey bars

¿Quieres probar las barras?
Do you want to try the monkey bars?

¿Te sientes seguro ahí?
Do you feel safe up there?

¿Quieres subir la escalera?
Do you want to climb the ladder?

¿Quieres cruzar la barra?
Do you want to walk across the balance beam?

¿Te has hecho daño?
Did you hurt yourself?
Did you get hurt?

Pupa/pupita Boo boo, ouchie

¡Preparados, listos, ya!
Ready, set, go!

¡Hasta luego, amigo!
See you later, friend!

Despegue/arranque
Blast off!

¡Uy, que torpe!
Oopsie Daisy!

Plof Pop!
As in a balloon or bubble

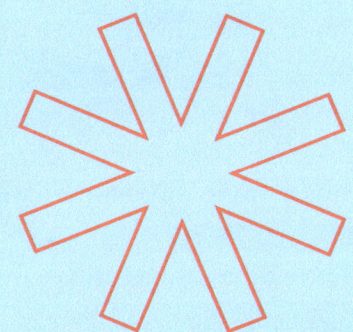

KIDS SONGS & LULLABIES

Canciones infantiles y nanas

"Un Elefante Se Balanceaba"
A fun Spanish song about elephants balancing on a spider web.

"Debajo un botón"
A classic Spanish nursery rhyme about a button found under a mushroom.

"Cucú, cantaba la rana"
A playful frog-themed song that helps children practice simple repeated syllables.

"El patio de mi casa"
A traditional song often accompanied by hand-holding and circling games.

"Pin Pon es un muñeco"
A popular rhyme about Pin Pon, the cardboard doll who teaches hygiene and good manners.

"Cochinitos dormilones"
Also known as "Los cochinitos," a lullaby about little piggies who go to sleep.

"Estrellita, dónde estás"
(Spanish version of Twinkle, Twinkle, Little Star)
A Spanish adaptation that helps toddlers recognize nighttime routines and stars.

"Cinco lobitos"
A finger-play rhyme counting from one to five with wolf cubs.

"Soy una taza" *(Cantajuego version)*
A catchy action song where children mimic being different kitchen items.

"La vaca Lola"
A very simple tune about a cow named Lola, popularized by children's YouTube channels in Spanish.

"Hola Don Pepito, Hola Don José"

KIDS CHARACTERS
Personajes Infantiles

Pollo Pepe:
A brightly colored, large-eyed chick from a popular picture book series.

Pocoyó:
A beloved animated character in a simple, educational cartoon aimed at toddlers.

Los Lunnis:
Puppet-like characters from a long-running Spanish children's TV show on RTVE.

Peppa Pig:
The Spanish-dubbed version of the British series is widely watched by Spanish toddlers.

Teo:
A character from Spanish children's books who explores everyday life and routines.

Caillou:
A Canadian-French character also dubbed into Spanish, popular on various children's networks.

D'Artacán y los tres mosqueperros:
A classic Spanish-Japanese cartoon adaptation of The Three Musketeers, with dog characters (though more recognized by slightly older kids, it still has nostalgic presence).

Los PJ Masks *(versión en español):*
Superhero kids in pajamas, popular on TV, and widely merchandise in Spain.

La Gallina Turuleca:
A character from a traditional Spanish song turned into a fun animated figure in modern versions.

SESAME STREET CHARACTERS

Personajes del Barrio Sésamo

Elmo Elmo

Triqui Cookie Monster
(sometimes also called el Monstruo de las Galletas)

Oscar el Gruñón Oscar the Grouch

Epi y Blas Bert and Ernie

Coco Grover

El Conde Draco Count von Count

The "Big Bird" equivalent went through different versions in Spain:

⟶ **Caponata - *1979 adaptation***: A large yellow-and-pink bird costume character *(instead of Big Bird)*

⟶ **Espinete - *1983 adaptation***: A big, friendly pink hedgehog who replaced Caponata and became one of the most iconic Barrio Sésamo characters for Spanish audiences

⟶ **Don Pimpón**: Another local character who often appeared alongside Espinete

Feeding and Mealtime

Alimentación y Hora de Comer

COMMON FOOD-RELATED PHRASES
Frases Comunes Relacionadas con la Comida

> «Barriguita llena, corazón contento»
> A common phrase after eating, meaning «Full tummy, happy heart»

'Ñam ñam Yum yum

¡Qué rico! Yummy

¡Puaj! Yucky

¡Ya está! All done

Los alimentos sólidos Solid foods

Estoy a tope I'm giving it my all

Masticar To chew

Tragar To swallow

Babero Bib

Biberón Baby bottle

El bol Bowl

El plato Plate

La taza Cup *(open)*

El termo Insulated tumbler

La pajita Straw

Leche en polvo Baby formula

No puedo más I'm full

Un bocado A bite

Tiquismiquis Picky

La fiambrera Lunch box

Las bolsitas de puré Puree pouches

La comida triturada Mashed food

Qué te apetece? What would you like?

Comilón/Comilona Someone who loves to eat

Merienda Snack

→ **Quieres una merienda?** Do you want a snack?

FEEDING TOOLS AND METHODS
Herramientas y Métodos para la Alimentación

El calienta biberones Bottle warmer

El sacaleches Breast pump

El asiento elevador Booster seat

La trona High chair

El esterilizador Sterilizer

La lactancia materna Breastfeeding

El recogemigas Crumb catcher

La taza de aprendizaje Sippy cup

KID-FRIENDLY FOODS – AMERICAN
Comidas para Niños – EEUU

Many of these foods are common for kids in the US, but many are not popular or widely available in Spain.

Los gofres Waffles

La paleta Popsicle

Los chuches Candy

Las gomitas Gummies

El pan de plátano Banana bread

Un rollo de canela Cinnamon roll

Los nuggets de pollo Chicken nuggets

Las albóndigas Meatballs

Los macarrones con queso Mac and cheese

Las bolsitas de puré Baby food pouches

Las bolsitas de yogur Yogurt pouches

La campota de manzana Apple sauce

Fruta en almíbar Fruit cups, preserved fruit

Un batido de frutas Fruit smoothie

Los huevos revueltos Scrambled eggs

Los guisantes y zanahorias Peas & carrots

Las rodajas de naranja Orange slices/wedges

Las tortitas con sirope de acre Pancakes with syrup

La pasta con mantequilla Buttered noodles

El bocadillo de queso fundido Grilled cheese sandwich

Los gajos de mandarina en almíbar ligero Mandarin slices in light syrup

Las magdalenas de arándano Blueberry muffins

El bocadillo de mantequilla de cacahuete y mermelada Peanut butter & jelly sandwich

El helado en cono con granas Ice cream cone with sprinkles

KID-FRIENDLY FOODS – SPAIN

Comidas para Niños – España

¿Cuáles comidas son los favoritos de niños españoles?

Bocadillos Sandwiches

Puré Bisque/Soup

Croquetas caseras Homemade croquettes

Tortilla de patatas. Spanish omelette with potatoes

Hamburguesas con patatas Burgers and fries

Chuches Candy

Tartas Cakes

Sopa de fideos Noodle soup

Churros con chocolate Sweet churros dipped in hot chocolate

Pan con nocilla Sandwich with chocolate-hazelnut spread *(Spain's answer to Nutella)*

Palitos de pan con queso Breadsticks with cheese spread

Espaguetis con tomate y chorizo Spaghetti with tomato sauce and chorizo

Albóndigas con patatas guisadas Meatballs with roasted potatoes

Arroz, tomate y huevo frito Rice with tomato sauce & a fried egg

Seasonal and Cultural Events

Eventos Estacionales y Culturales

BIRTHDAYS
Los Cumpleaños

Cumpleañero/a Birthday boy/girl

Globos Balloons

Fiesta de cumpleaños Birthday party

Invitados Guests

Disfraz Costume

Torta de cumpleaños Birthday cake

Payaso Clown

Velas Candles

Juegos de fiesta Party games

The happy birthday song

Cumpleaños feliz, cumpleaños feliz, te deseamos [nombre], un cumpleaños feliz!

HALLOWEEN

Disfraz Costume

Bolsa de dulces Trick or treat bag

Tocar el timbre. Ring the bell

Calabazas Pumpkins

Gomitas Gummies

Ir a pedir dulces To go trick or treating

Dulces Candy

Chuches Candy

"Truco o trato" "Trick or treat"

ChupaChups Lollipop
ChupaChups is a Barcelona-based brand and the brand name is often used as the general term for any lollipop of any brand.

Piruleta Lollipop

Casa encantada Haunted house

Toc toc Knock knock

Linterna de calabaza Jack-o'-lantern

Din don Ding dong

Tocar el timbre Ring the doorbell

La entrada The driveway

Tela de araña Spiderweb

CHRISTMAS AND THE THREE KINGS
La Navidad y Los Reyes Magos

La nochebuena Christmas Eve

Los adornos Ornaments

La pista de hielo Ice rink

El belén Nativity scene

El encendido de luces Tree lighting ceremony

Luces de navidad Christmas lights

La corona de navidad Christmas wreath

Villancicos Christmas carols

El muñeco de nieve Snowman

El copo de nieve Snowflake

El elfo mago, o el elfo en la estantería Elf on the Shelf

El patinaje sobre hielo Ice skating

Turrón Nougat
(a Christmas staple in Spain)

El calendario de adviento Advent calendar

GIFTING
Regalos

El lazo Bow

El intercambio de regalos Gift exchange

El papel de regalo Wrapping paper

Las detalles Stocking stuffers
Detalles just refers to little gifts in general but a more direct translation does not exist

El amigo invisible Secret santa

MUSIC
La Música

El cascabel Jingle bell

Los villancicos Christmas carols

SANTA CLAUS
Papá Noel

Papá Noel Santa Claus

El trineo Sleigh

Los renos Reindeer

La lista de regalos Gift list

El árbol de Navidad Christmas tree

Sentarse en el regazo de Papa Noel To sit in Santa's lap

El polo norte The North Pole

Las luces navideñas Christmas lights

El calcetín navideño Christmas stocking

Portarse bien o no, travieso o bien portado Naughty or nice

El reno de nariz roja Red-nosed reindeer

El saco de regalos Bag of presents

El sombrero de Papá Noel Santa hat

Los ayudantes de Papá Noel Santa's helpers

HOLIDAY TREATS
Chuches Navideñas

Las castañas Chestnuts
Fresh roasted chestnuts are a common street food in Spain during the holidays

Los pastones Candy canes

El roscón de reyes A traditional wreath-shaped cake served in Spain at Christmas
You typically hide a small figurine representing the baby Jesus, along with a dried fava bean; the person who finds the figurine is considered «king» for the day, while whoever finds the bean usually has to pay for the next year's roscón.

El mazapán Marzipan

El polvorón Shortbread cookie

El turrón Nougat

Los mantecados Traditional Spanish Christmas shortbread sweets

El bizcocho de jengibre Gingerbread

El azúcar glas Powdered sugar

THREE KINGS DAY
Día de los Reyes

Día de los Reyes The Epiphany
January 6, the day the Reyes Magos typically "visit" – people leave their shoes out and the Reyes leave presents in each family member's shoes

La cabalgata de los Reyes Magos
The parade celebrating the arrival of the Three Wise Men

Los reyes [magos]
The 3 kings / the 3 wise men

¿QUÉ ES EL DÍA DE LOS REYES?

En España, después de la Navidad, celebramos **una fiesta muy especial** que se llama el **Día de los Reyes Magos**, el 6 de enero.

¿Sabes quiénes son los Reyes Magos?

Son **tres señores muy sabios** que se llaman Melchor, Gaspar y Baltasar. Viajaron desde muy lejos siguiendo una estrella para llevar regalos a un bebé muy especial.

Ahora, cada año, **los Reyes Magos traen regalos a los niños buenos**, como hace Papá Noel.

La noche del 5 de enero, **los niños dejan sus zapatos** en un lugar visible, como cerca de la puerta o del árbol de Navidad. También preparamos algo para los Reyes y sus camellos, como **agua y galletas**.

Cuando te despiertas el día 6 de enero, ¡encontrarás regalos al lado de tus zapatos! Es **un día mágico**, lleno de sorpresas y alegría.

Además, ese día comemos un dulce especial que se llama **Roscón de Reyes**, que tiene frutas por encima y, a veces, un regalito escondido dentro.

¡Si encuentras el regalito, dicen que eres **el rey o la reina** por un día!

¿No es una tradición preciosa?

¿Qué te gustaría pedirles a los Reyes Magos este año?

NEW YEAR'S EVE
La noche vieja

Nochevieja New Years Eve

La cuenta atrás Countdown

Las campanadas Chimes from the clock at midnight

Champin: an alcohol-free drink kids drink on New Years Eve; it's in a yellow bottle with a clown on it

Tomar las uvas To eat grapes

En España, la última noche del año, que se llama **Nochevieja**, tenemos una una **tradición muy divertida** y especial.

Cuando el reloj marca la medianoche y empieza un nuevo año, **las personas comen doce uvas**, ¡una por cada campanada del reloj! Cada vez que escuchamos "¡DING!", comemos una uva.

¿Por qué hacemos esto?

Porque dicen que si comes las doce uvas a tiempo, tendrás **suerte y felicidad** durante los doce meses del año. Es como un pequeño juego, pero también un deseo de **cosas buenas** para el año nuevo.

¡Es **muy gracioso** porque algunas personas se ríen mucho tratando de no atragantarse con tantas uvas!

¿Te gustaría probarlo este año conmigo?

Phrases to Guide Kids Behavior

Frases para guiar el comportamiento infantil

BASIC BEHAVIORAL VOCABULARY

Vocabulario básico del comportamiento infantil

Hacer pucheritos
To pout *(adorably)*

Zapatear To stomp

Arañar To scratch

Lloriquear To whine

Cabrearse To get very angry

Levantar los ojos al cielo
To roll your eyes

Una rabieta Meltdown

⟶ **Si no hace siesta pronto, tendrá una rabieta**
If he doesn't nap soon, he will have a meltdown

Tener un berrinche
To have a temper tantrum

De la noche a la mañana
Overnight, really quickly
"Raquel empezó a caminar de la noche a la mañana". Raquel learned to walk overnight.

El que tiene boca, se equivoca
Everyone makes mistakes! It's natural

Las cosas de palacio van despacio.
Good things take time. Rome wasn't built in a day

¡No es moco de paco! Don't take it lightly, it's more important than it seems

MANAGING TOUGH SITUATIONS
Navegando situaciónes difíciles

De ninguna manera
Absolutely not

Lo digo en serio I mean it

Eso es para los papás That's for grown-ups *(como el café)*

No me no me, que te que te
Don't try me, or else

Te has pasado tres pueblos
You've crossed the line

Ajo y agua Deal with it

Baja la voz, cari
Quiet down, sweety

Necesito espacio. Dame 5 minutos y volvemos a jugar.
I need space. Give me 5 minutes and then we'll play some more.

Voz de interior, por favor
Inside voice, please

Usa la voz bajita
Use your quiet (inside) voice

Dime con palabras, no con gritos
Tell me with words, not shouts

¿Necesitas un momento para calmarte? Do you need a moment to calm down?

WORDS OF AFFIRMATION
Palabras de Afirmación

Soy fuerte
Soy creativa
Soy paciente

Eres valiente You are brave

Eres amable You are kind

Eres fuerte You are strong

Eres inteligente You are smart

Eres creativa You are creative

Eres gracioso You are funny

Eres paciente You are patient

Eres capaz You are capable

"Te quiero muchísimo"
«I love you so much»

"Eres mi persona favorita en el mundo"
«You're my favorite person in the world»

"Siempre estaré aquí para cuidarte"
«I'll always be here to take care of you»

"Me hace muy feliz estar contigo"
«Being with you makes me so happy»

"Eres muy importante para mí"
«You're very important to me»

"Puedes hacerlo, eres muy capaz"
«You can do it, you're very capable»

"Inténtalo, estoy aquí para ayudarte"
«Try it, I'm here to help you»

"Es normal equivocarse, aprenderás poco a poco"
«It's normal to make mistakes; you'll learn little by little»

"Estoy muy orgullosa/o de ti"
«I'm so proud of you»

"Tienes un corazón muy bonito"
«You have a beautiful heart»

"Eres muy curioso, y eso es genial"
«You're very curious, and that's great»

"Me encanta cómo usas tu imaginación"
«I love how you use your imagination»

"Eres muy especial, no hay nadie como tú"
«You're very special; there's no one like you»

ESTABLISHING CLEAR EXPECTATIONS

Estableciendo expectativas claras

⟶ **"Los juguetes se quedan en el suelo, no los tiramos"**
«Toys stay on the floor; we don't throw them»

⟶ **"Las manos suaves son para acariciar, no para golpear"**
«Gentle hands are for touching, not for hitting»

⟶ **"Es hora de recoger. ¿Quieres empezar con los bloques o los coches?"**
«It's time to clean up. Do you want to start with the blocks or the cars?»

⟶ **"Aquí caminamos despacio, no corremos"**
«Here we walk slowly; we don't run»

⟶ **"Las cosas se piden con palabras, no con gritos"**
«We ask for things with words, not by shouting»

⟶ **"Los libros son para leer, no para romper"**
«Books are for reading, not for tearing»

⟶ **"En la mesa, nos sentamos y comemos tranquilos"**
«At the table, we sit and eat calmly»

⟶ **"Para cruzar la calle, siempre damos la mano"**
«To cross the street, we always hold hands»

RECOGNIZING EMOTIONS
Reconociendo las emociones

⟶ **"Entiendo que estes enfadado, pero no gritamos. Puedes usar palabras"**
«I understand you're upset, but we don't scream. You can use words»

⟶ **"Estás triste porque no quieres compartir. Es difícil, pero podemos intentar juntos"**
«You're sad because you don't want to share. It's hard, but we can try together»

⟶ **"Veo que estás frustrado. Vamos a respirar hondo juntos"**
«I see you're frustrated. Let's take a deep breath together»

⟶ **"Veo que estás muy cansado. A veces eso nos pone un poco gruñones"**
«I see you're very tired. Sometimes that makes us a little grumpy»

⟶ **"Sé que te sientes frustrado porque no puedes hacerlo. Vamos a intentarlo juntos"**
«I know you're frustrated because you can't do it. Let's try together»

⟶ **"Entiendo que querías jugar más, pero es hora de recoger"**
«I understand you wanted to play more, but it's time to clean up»

⟶ **"Es difícil compartir, pero podemos practicar eso juntos"**
«It's hard to share, but we can practice it together»

⟶ **"¿Estás enfadado? Está bien estarlo. ¿Quieres un abrazo?"**
«Are you angry? It's okay to feel that way. Do you want a hug?»

REDIRECTING BEHAVIOR
Redirigiendo el comportamiento

⟶ **"No podemos pintar en la pared, pero sí en este papel"**
«We can't paint on the wall, but we can paint on this paper»

⟶ **"No mordemos a las personas. Si necesitas morder algo, usa este mordedor"**
«We don't bite people. If you need to bite something, use this teether»

⟶ **"La mesa no es para saltar, pero podemos saltar en el suelo"**
«The table is not for jumping, but we can jump on the floor»

⟶ **"Las manos no son para pegar, son para jugar y dar abrazos"**
«Hands are not for hitting; they're for playing and giving hugs»

⟶ **"Las paredes no se pintan, pero podemos pintar este dibujo tan bonito"**
«We don't paint on the walls, but we can paint this beautiful picture»

⟶ **"La comida no se tira. Si ya no tienes hambre, dime"**
«We don't throw food. If you're not hungry anymore, tell me»

⟶ **"Las voces altas son para fuera. Dentro usamos voces tranquilas"**
«Loud voices are for outside. Inside, we use calm voices»

⟶ **"Si necesitas descargar energía, vamos a saltar aquí en lugar de en el sofá"**
«If you need to burn some energy, let's jump here instead of on the couch»

REINFORCING GOOD BEHAVIOR

Reforzando el buen comportamiento

→ **"¡Gracias por usar tus palabras para pedir ayuda!"**
«Thank you for using your words to ask for help!»

→ **"Mira qué bien estás esperando tu turno, ¡muy paciente!"**
«You're doing a great job waiting your turn, so patient!»

→ **"Me encanta cómo estás recogiendo tus juguetes. ¡Sigue así!"**
«I love how you're picking up your toys. Keep it up!»

→ **"Qué bien has esperado tu turno, estoy muy orgullosa/o de ti"**
«You waited your turn so well; I'm very proud of you»

→ **"Gracias por guardar tus juguetes, ¡has hecho un gran trabajo!"**
«Thank you for putting away your toys; you did a great job!»

→ **"Me gusta cómo estás escuchando con atención"**
«I like how you're listening carefully»

→ **¡Qué amable has sido al compartir con tu amigo!"**
«How kind you've been to share with your friend!»

→ **"Has hecho un esfuerzo enorme, y eso es lo más importante"**
«You've made such a big effort, and that's what matters most»

CALM CONSEQUENCES
Consecuencias tranquilas

⟶ **"Si sigues tirando los juguetes, voy a tener que guardarlos"**
«If you keep throwing the toys, I'll have to put them away»

⟶ **"Ahora vamos a esperar un ratito para calmarnos antes de volver a jugar"**
«Now we're going to take a moment to calm down before playing again»

⟶ **"La pintura está almacenada porque no la usamos de manera correcta. La probaremos más tarde"**
«The paint is put away because we didn't use it correctly. We'll try again later»

⟶ **"Si sigues gritando, vamos a hacer una pausa para calmarnos"**
«If you keep shouting, we'll take a break to calm down»

⟶ **"El juguete se guarda ahora porque no lo estamos usando correctamente"**
«The toy will be put away now because we're not using it correctly»

⟶ **"Si corres aquí dentro, puedes caerte y hacerte daño. Por eso necesitamos caminar"**
«If you run in here, you might fall and hurt yourself. That's why we need to walk»

⟶ **"Cuando estemos tranquilos, podemos volver a jugar"**
«When we're calm, we can go back to playing»

⟶ **"Ahora vamos a pensar en lo que pasó y cómo podemos hacerlo mejor la próxima vez"**
«Now we're going to think about what happened and how we can do it better next time»

ENCOURAGE REFLECTION
Fomentando la reflexión

→ **"¿Cómo crees que se sintió tu amigo cuando le pegaste?"**
«How do you think your friend felt when you hit them?»

→ **"Vamos a intentar otra vez, ¿cómo podemos hacerlo diferente?"**
«Let's try again; how can we do it differently?»

→ **¿Cómo podrías pedir el juguete en lugar de arrebatárselo?"**
«How could you ask for the toy instead of grabbing it?»

→ **"¿Por qué crees que tu amigo está triste? ¿Qué podemos hacer para ayudar?"**
«Why do you think your friend is sad? What can we do to help?»

→ **"¿Cómo podemos evitar que pase otra vez?"**
«How can we prevent this from happening again?»

→ **"¿Qué más podrías hacer si estás enfadado en lugar de gritar?"**
«What else could you do if you're angry instead of shouting?»

→ **"Cuando haces eso, ¿cómo crees que se sienten los demás?"**
«When you do that, how do you think others feel?»

"¿Qué podemos hacer para arreglar esto?"
«What can we do to fix this?»

EMPATHY & CONNECTION
Empatía y conexión

⟶ **"Sé que querías ese juguete. Vamos a pensar cómo compartirlo"**
«I know you wanted that toy. Let's think about how to share it»

⟶ **"Te cuesta esperar, lo sé. ¿Quieres que juguemos algo mientras tanto?"**
«It's hard for you to wait, I know. Do you want to play something in the meantime?»

⟶ **"Tú puedes hacerlo, y yo estoy aquí para ayudarte"**
«You can do it, and I'm here to help you»

⟶ **"Sé que querías ese juguete. Es difícil esperar, pero yo estoy aquí contigo"**
«I know you wanted that toy. It's hard to wait, but I'm here with you»

⟶ **"Sé que estás cansado. Vamos a sentarnos juntos un rato"**
«I know you're tired. Let's sit together for a while»

⟶ **"¿Te gustaría un abrazo grande para sentirte mejor?"**
«Would you like a big hug to feel better?»

⟶ **"Entiendo que te cueste compartir, pero me gusta que lo estés intentando"**
«I understand sharing is hard for you, but I like that you're trying»

⟶ **"Todos tenemos días difíciles. Lo importante es que siempre lo intentamos otra vez"**
«We all have hard days. The important thing is that we always try again»

APOLOGIZING

Más opciones para decir "lo siento"

Fue un error mío It was my mistake

Siento haber dicho eso Sorry I said that

Me arrepiento I regret that

Lo retiro I take it all back

No quería hacerte daño
I didn't mean to hurt you

Volvería atrás en el tiempo, pero no puedo
I would go back in time, but I can't

Me he equivocado I made a mistake

Me perdonas? Will you forgive me?

Metí la pata I messed up

La he liado I messed up

MANAGING TANTRUMS
Navegando Rabietas

⟶ **"Veo que estás muy enfadado. ¿Quieres contarme qué pasa?"**
«I see you're really upset. Do you want to tell me what's going on?»

⟶ **"Entiendo que quieras seguir jugando, pero es hora de parar"**
«I understand that you want to keep playing, but it's time to stop»

⟶ **"¿Te apetece un abrazo para sentirte mejor?"**
«Do you want a hug to feel better?»

⟶ **"Vamos a respirar hondo juntos. Inhala... exhala..."**
«Let's take a deep breath together. Inhale... exhale...»

⟶ **"Si estás enfadado, podemos zapatear o apretar un cojín"**
«If you're angry, we can stomp our feet or squeeze a pillow»

⟶ **"Puedes decirme con palabras lo que te molesta"**
«You can tell me with words what's bothering you»

⟶ **"Sé que es difícil, pero podemos encontrar otra cosa divertida para hacer"**
«I know it's hard, but we can find something else fun to do»

⟶ **"Cuando estés listo, podemos hablar de lo que pasó"**
«When you're ready, we can talk about what happened»

⟶ **"Sé que estás triste, pero no podemos tirar cosas. Vamos a guardarlas"**
«I know you're sad, but we can't throw things. Let's put them away»

⟶ **"Podemos seguir hablando cuando estemos más tranquilos"**
«We can keep talking when we're calmer»

BEDTIME STRUGGLES
Dificultades a la Hora de Dormir

1. Crear una rutina clara

"Ahora toca recoger los juguetes, después bañito y luego pijama"
«Now it's time to put away the toys, then bath time, and then pajamas»

"¿Qué canción te apetece cantar antes de dormir?"
«Which song would you like to sing before bed?»

2. Ofrecer elección en las tareas

"¿Quieres ponerte el pijama azul o el rojo?"
«Do you want to wear the blue or the red pajamas?»

"¿Prefieres beber agua antes o después de lavarte los dientes?"
«Do you want to drink water before or after brushing your teeth?»

3. Uso de un tono tranquilizador

"El día ha sido muy largo, es el momento de descansar para sentirnos mejor mañana"
«It has been a long day; it's time to rest so we feel better tomorrow»

"Te quiero mucho. Estaré cerquita si me necesitas"
«I love you so much. I'll be close by if you need me»

4. Validar el miedo o la inquietud

"¿Hay algo que te preocupa? ¿Quieres contármelo?"
«Are you worried about something? Do you want to tell me?»

"A veces da miedo la oscuridad, pero yo estoy aquí contigo"
«Sometimes the dark is scary, but I'm here with you»

5. Mantener la calma y la consistencia

"Es normal no querer dormir todavía, pero nuestro cuerpo necesita descansar"
«It's normal not to want to sleep yet, but our body needs to rest»

"Vamos a cerrar los ojitos. Mañana podremos jugar de nuevo"
«Let's close our eyes. Tomorrow we can play again»

Recetas para la familia

PAN CON TOMATE

1. **Put the tomato** and the blender. You can either toss the garlic in too, or rub it on the bread.

2. **Spoon the blended tomato** onto your bread.

3. **Drizzle with a bit of oil**, sprinkle with salt and pepper to taste, and **top with ham or proscuitto**.

This dish is commonly enjoyed at breakfast, though you'll likely find it on the menu any time of day.

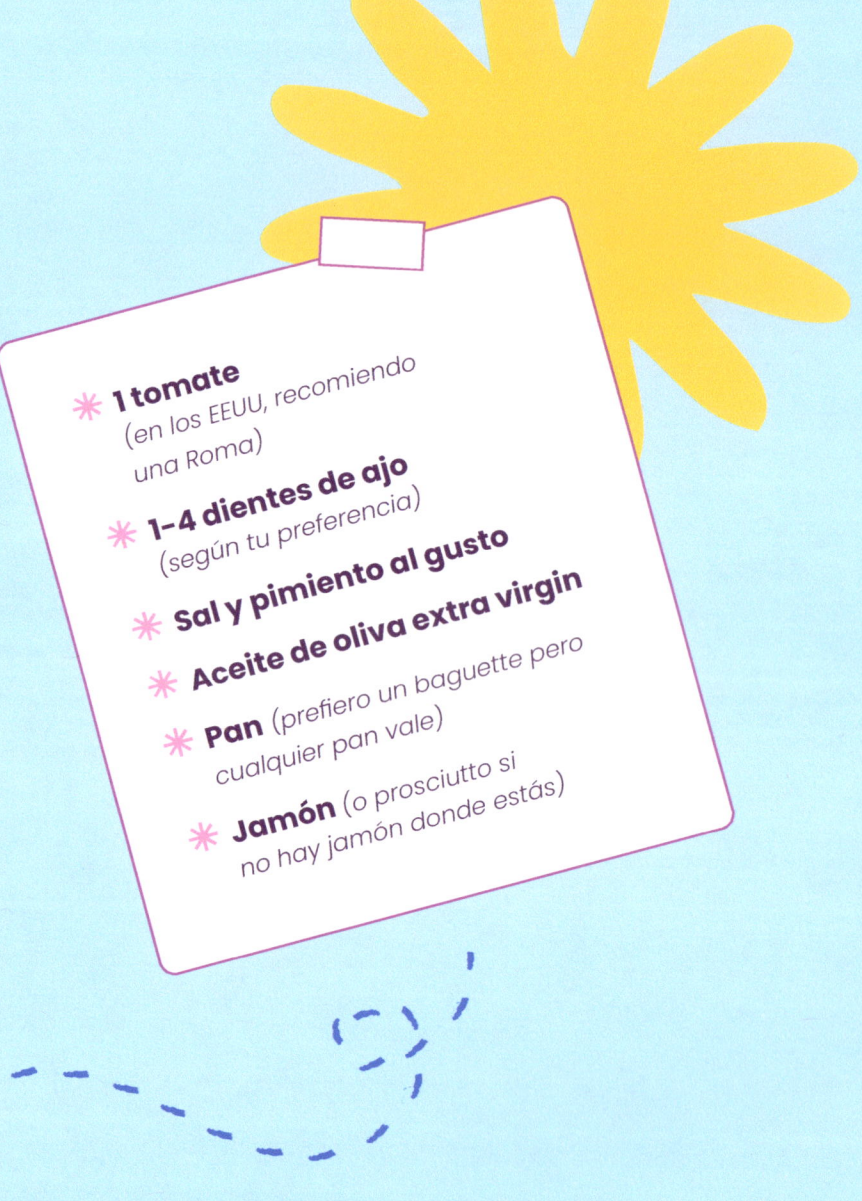

- **1 tomate** (en los EEUU, recomiendo una Roma)
- **1-4 dientes de ajo** (según tu preferencia)
- **Sal y pimiento al gusto**
- **Aceite de oliva extra virgin**
- **Pan** (prefiero un baguette pero cualquier pan vale)
- **Jamón** (o prosciutto si no hay jamón donde estás)

PUREE DE CALABAZA Y ZANAHORIA

- **1 cup pumpkin or squash, peeled and chopped**
- **2 carrots, peeled and chopped**
- **½ onion, peeled and diced**
- **1 potato** (optional)
- **1 teaspoon extra virgin olive oil**
- **Dash of salt** (optional)

1. Prepare the vegetables. **Place the vegetables in a pot** and fill it with enough water to cover the vegetables.

2. **Boil the vegetables** for about 20 minutes. Alternatively, you could pan roast the vegetables in a pan on medium heat until they've softened.

3. Remove the vegetables with a slotted spoon and place in the blender. **Blend, adding more water** until it reaches your desired consistency.

Tip: You can add in other vegetables you may have on hand, such as leeks or zucchini.

TORTILLA ESPAÑOLA AL ESTILO MAMÁ

* **3 medium potatoes peeled and sliced thin or roughly chopped** (ideally Yukon Gold if you're in the US)

* **4 eggs, beaten**

* **Extra virgin olive oil**

* **Salt and pepper to taste**

1. Heat enough oil in a pan to **cover the potatoes**. Add potatoes, season with salt and pepper, and cook the potatoes covered on low heat.

2. Once the potatoes are very soft, remove the lid and turn up the heat to **brown potatoes a bit**. Remove potatoes with a slotted spoon.

3. **Mix potatoes and egg together**, season with salt and pepper.

4. Drain most of the oil, leaving a little in the pan so the tortilla doesn't stick to it. **Pour the egg and potato mixture into the pan** and cook on medium heat.

5. Run the spatula between the pan and the mixture to help form the edges and prevent sticking. When the mixture appears about half cooked, **it's time to flip it**.

6. Get a large plate or charger, and place it on top of the pan and flip it quickly, then **quickly slide the mixture back onto the pan**. The done side of the tortilla should look cooked and slightly browned.

7. Continue to run the spatula along the edges of the tortilla. Once cooked through, **transfer the tortilla to a plate** and enjoy.

Worried about flipping the tortilla? Practice first!

Tip

Reddit user u/chroniclerofblarney recommends this:

"Make a **flat layer of unpeeled bananas** in a cold frying pan. Place a large dinner plate, eating side down, on top of the bananas.

Practice flipping the pan upside down while holding the dinner plate with your other hand.

Do that three times and you'll never worry about flipping a tortilla. Most people find this technique difficult with a hot ass pan full of cooked potatoes, but if you just do it a couple of times **you'll be totally fine** when you try it with hot stuff."

Still worried about the flip? Another reddit user, u/boollish, recommends this:

"What I do is **slide it off onto a rimmed plate**, cooked side down. Then put **two rimmed plates together** and flip it, and slide the result back into the pan.

It doesn't look as pretty, but **it's a lot easier** to get the job done."

HUEVOS ROTOS

1. Prepare the french fries according to the package instructions in the oven or air fryer. Alternatively, **peel and cut potatoes in wedges** or large chunks and fry them in oil until golden.

2. **Fry the eggs.**

3. When the fries or potatoes are ready, put them in a bowl or serving dish. **Top the fries with the egg and ham.**

4. **Break the yolks**, mix it all up, serve, and enjoy!

* 1 small bag of frozen french fries, or 4 medium potatoes
* 2 eggs
* **Spanish ham, diced** (or prosciutto if Spanish ham isn't available. I've even used diced American ham in this recipe)
* **Salt and pepper to taste**

This is a very simplified version of a classic dish.

There are more homemade and delicious ways to prepare the potatoes, but this is meant to be a quick & easy weeknight version when you're short on time.

CARNE NAVIDEÑA AL ESTILO URSULA

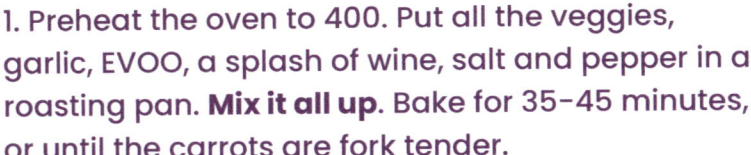

My Spanish "mom" makes this every year for Christmas, and now I do as well.

* **1/2 pound carrots, peeled and roughly chopped in medium size pieces** *(like the size of potatoes for tortilla)*
* **1 big yellow onion, peeled and roughly chopped in chunks**
* **Garlic**
* **Extra virgin olive oil**
* **Salt and pepper to taste**
* **A splash of sherry or wine**
* **3 pounds sirloin steak** *(you can cook as much as you need for your group; the sauce goes a long way)*

1. Preheat the oven to 400. Put all the veggies, garlic, EVOO, a splash of wine, salt and pepper in a roasting pan. **Mix it all up**. Bake for 35-45 minutes, or until the carrots are fork tender.

2. **Add beef on top of the veggies** and bake until it's cooked. This dish is best if the beef is cooked until it's rare. This should take about 10 minutes.

3. Remove the pan from the oven. Let the meat rest. **Pour the contents of the pan into a blender** and blend.

4. **Spoon the carrot sauce over the meat** & enjoy!

Appendix

THE 3 RULES OF PRONUNCIATION

Do you ever wonder if you're pronouncing a word in Spanish correctly?

One of the most influential teachers I have ever had was incredibly strict, and a bit unorthodox. A lot of people would probably describe him, Dr. Finkelstein, as a prickly and eccentric personality. He was indeed, and I really liked him. His blunt and militaristic approach to learning Spanish was effective for me.

Dr Finkelstein hammered home **two concepts that really accelerated my speech proficiency** in Spanish.

First and foremost, in Spanish, **vowels make one (and only one) sound**, unlike English.

He repeated this phrase to help us memorize each vowel's sound:

A E I O U, el burro sabe más que tú
[A E I O U, a donkey knows more than you].

Spelled phonetically, that would sound like **"ah, ay, ee, oh, ooo, el burro sabe más que tú."**

He also required his students to memorize these **three simple rules of pronunciation** that totally changed the game for me:

✳ Si una **palabra termina con vocal, n, o s,** el acento natural cae en la penúltima sílaba.

✳ Si una **palabra termina con consonante, menos n o s,** el acento natural cae en la última sílaba.

✳ Si una **palabra no sigue regla 1 o 2,** tendrá un acento escrito.

When the rule says where the accent falls, that means that's where the tone of your voice should go up.

Example: Lápiz is pronounced LAH-peace, not lah-PEACE.

When we'd pronounce a word wrong, he would stop us mid-sentence and require us to **recite the Three Rules**, and then pronounce the original word correctly. It wasn't uncommon for us to spend half a class this way. If you or someone you know struggles with pronunciation, **I highly recommend memorizing these rules**.

The summer after I learned the Three Rules, I studied abroad in Spain (San Sebastián) for the first time. I somehow left my digital camera just inside the locked door to the vestibule of the building where I was living, and for some reason didn't have my key.

I saw a neighbor and tried pointing to my camera and asked for their help to get it.

"Mi camera! Mi camera!" They looked at me perplexed, and **had no idea what I was saying.**

Finally, I remembered that camera is spelled "cámera" which means (thanks to rule no. 3) I need my intonation to go up on the A. I repeated the word while applying rule no. 3 and **BOOM, my neighbor understood me** (and helped me get my camera).

I have tried with no success to find Dr. Finkelstein so I could write to him and share some stories with him about how **his lessons continue to help me to this day**.

He repeatedly implored his students to never drop by the school to say hi to him after we graduate.

One day, a graduate interrupted class to pop his head in and say hi, and I still remember how annoyed our teacher was.

So, instead of continuing to try to track him down to offer my gratitude, **I'm sharing his lessons with you**.

MY FAVORITE SOCIAL MEDIA RESOURCES

These recommendations were compiled in January 2025. The availability and names of this accounts may change over time.

Below are the accounts I follow that have been a tremendous help for me. I follow them on Instagram, but I know many of them are also active on other platforms.

@_anagildersleeve: A Valencian woman who married an American, Ana and her husband are raising their family in Kansas (where I live)! She taught me one of my favorite new terms: **no te no te, que te que te!** This loosely translates to "**don't try me, or else!**" Ana shares a lot of great videos about raising her own kids to be bilingual, Spanish sayings and customs, and more.

@mamaenmadrid & **@mothereuro**: Emily, also known as Mamá en Madrid, is an Oregonian who worked as an au pair in Madrid where she met her now husband. They lived in the U.S. for a bit before building their life in Madrid. She launched Mother Euro to **help families who plan to relocate to Europe** and need help navigating the logistics of doing so.

Maryam, better known as @spanishteacher_madrid, has a PhD in teaching Spanish and has two decades of doing so. Hers is one of my favorite accounts for learning more advanced colloquialisms.

Many of her videos follow the format of her introducing a new term and then showing clips of the term being used in pop culture. A otra cosa, mariposa is a term I learned from her that means **"Next subject, please! Let's move on to something else!"** Another one I use often is **él que tiene boca, se equivoca**, or everyone makes mistakes!

Below are more accounts that I follow to continuously learn more. I've picked up really helpful tips and terms from all of them, many of which appear in this book!

@ninos.and.nature
@directespanol
@bilinguitos
@spanish.with.conchita
@holamydailyspanish
@espanolenpijama
@angela_spanish_online
@spanish.with.vicky
@spanishonline_
@spanish.takeaway

Travel Tips: Spain with kids

TIMING

My favorite time to visit Spain is in **September**. I usually split my time between Madrid and somewhere beach-y since **travel within Spain (and Europe) is cheap and easy**. San Sebastián, Alicante, and Menorca are some of my favorites.

Many Spaniards vacation for some or all of August. It's peak travel time, so prices for travel and lodging are the highest in August. If you're wanting to spend time in Madrid with less bustle, then **August is your best bet**, though it'll likely be really hot and humid.

PARKS, PARKS, PARKS

It wasn't until I became a parent that I noticed that **these parks are everywhere**.

Before my first trip to Spain with my daughter, Ana Gildersleeve posted to Instagram about how it's common in Spain for parks to be adjacent to bars/restaurants. She said it's common for parents to **let their kids play while they socialize with other parents**. I found this to be true and really fun for both my daughter and myself.

DINING

I've found restaurants in Spain to be **very kid-friendly**. Whether at fine dining restaurants or at a more casual spot, I've only had good experiences at restaurants with my daughter. High chairs and boosters are usually readily available. If there isn't an explicit kid menu, **restaurants have been very accommodating**. I've even been to nice restaurants that have designated play areas for kids.

Ask locals for restaurant recommendations. I've had a lot more luck asking locals than Googling. Here's the type of question I ask (people on the street, concierges, whoever): Busco un restaurante con comida típica española. Un restaurante donde coma la gente de aquí, no los turistas.

You can find global cuisines in Spain, but I'd recommend skipping them. It is a fun experience to go to a Mexican or Chinese restaurant, for example, because they're so different than what we experience at home. But if you're not in Spain for an extended period of time, I'd recommend focusing on restaurants that specialize in **dishes unique to the autonomous regions of Spain**.

When you're in the U.S. and think of Maine, you think of lobster. New Orleans? Beignets and gumbo. Even though Spain is a much smaller country, you'll find **plenty of diversity** in their regional cuisines as well. If you day trip to Segovia or Pedraza from Madrid, seek out cordero. In Valencia? Arroz (paella). Asturias? Fabada. País Vasco? Txakolí & tapas with seafood. Andalucia? Gazpacho and salmorejo (I love white gazpacho).

When in doubt, ask. I've generally found locals to be helpful and accommodating, especially if you use a script like this: **"Busco un restaurante que sirve platos típicos de esta región. ¿Hay alguno que me recomienda?"**

WHAT I STOCK UP ON IN SPAIN

Kids Books: Shopping for kids books in Spain is a totally different (and better) experience than shopping for books in Spanish in the United States. **Books are inexpensive** and there are so many incredible ones that simply aren't available outside of the country (yes, even on Amazon).

While I have used Amazon.com to buy translated versions of classic children's books, our favorite books have been unique ones we found in Spanish bookstores. If a trip to Spain is not in your near future, and you're willing to pay for pricey shipping, shopping **Amazon.es offers a better variety of books** in Spanish than Amazon.com.

Clothes: In my experience, shopping for kids clothes in Spain is so fun. You can get **really good quality** for Target prices.

My favorite shops include **Zara** (prices are half of what you'd pay if you order the same items from Zara in the U.S.), **Mango**, and **El Corte Inglés**. **Mayoral** is a popular chain of children's clothing stores. There are great boutiques with finer items as well.

@mamainmadrid_ offers a lot of great children's clothing recommendations in Madrid.

Mango
El Corte Inglés
Mayoral

Travel wipes: Most travel wipe packs in the U.S. are on the larger side, and are often too big for my purse. Sometimes I just want a **small Tic-Tac-sized pack** to put in my purse with a single diaper, and these are readily available in Spain. I usually get them at grocery stores.

Kids perfume: It's common in Spain for people to spritz their children's clothes with perfume as part of their "getting ready" routine at home or at daycare. You'll find **baby and kids perfumes** in the kids section of popular stores like Zara and Mango.

TRANSPORTATION

Car seats in airplanes: When my daughter was really young (~0-3 years old), I brought a carseat on the plane for her. I got a **"travel carseat"** on Facebook marketplace for $20. Airlines will require the car seat to be in a **window seat** (I learned this the hard way), and my daughter slept like a dream in it. She was so **much more comfortable** than she would have been sitting in the seat like an adult. Be sure to run the safety belt through the appropriate part of the carseat, or your little one may tip themselves out of it mid-snooze like mine did on our first trip.

Taxis will transport you and your little one around town **without a car seat if you're not going on highways**, but of course put safety first and either bring your own car seat or follow my next tip.

Taxis & Cabify: Cabify is an app like Uber. You can schedule a ride in advance and **specify that the car must have a car seat**. I had really mixed experiences with this service, to be honest. It worked the best when we knew we needed to catch a flight or train and could schedule it ahead of time.

In the future, I'll take a tip from my Spanish mom and **just call a cab service** on the phone. Calling a cab by phone was quick, easy, and could always accommodate a car seat request.

Strollers are very common in Spain. However, restaurants and stores are not always as spacious as in the U.S., so consider **a compact travel stroller**. Though our UppaBaby drives like a dream on Spanish cobblestone roads, it's impossible to accommodate in most restaurants because it's so big. My daughter's preference (and often my own) is for me to carry her around town in a **baby harness** when possible. It's so much easier for us to navigate public transport, shops and restaurants this way.

MEDICAL AID

I have limited experience in this area, but will share what I know: **Spanish pharmacies are everywhere**, and inexpensive. Look for a green neon cross; they hang over pharmacy doors.

My daughter has some medical complexities and I found myself needing to find her a specific medication on our first visit. It was readily available over the counter, and **at a fraction of the price as in the U.S**.

Spanish has a public healthcare system, though many Spaniards also have supplemental private insurance. If you're like me and find yourself needing an ER or urgent care, don't worry. They'll treat you, and **it won't cost the equivalent of college tuition**.

One year I went to Spain, I burned my forearm on my electric stovetop the night before my flight.

As you'd imagine, the burn got worse over the next few days. I ended up at urgent care to **properly treat and dress the burn**, and it cost me a grand total of $125.

(The nurse specifically told me not to go to the beach, which I assured her I would not do, and then I ran into her the next day at a beach restaurant where she reiterated her advice and laughed a bit about me toeing the line!)

NOTES

MY GO-TO SPANISH PHRASES

www.ingramcontent.com/pod-product-compliance
Lightning Source LLC
Chambersburg PA
CBHW050849010526

44107CB00018BA/1228